WISH UPON A STAR

A Story for Children With a Parent Who Is Mentally Ill

by Pamela L. Laskin and
Addie Alexander Moskowitz, C.S.W.

illustrated by Margo Lemieux

MAGINATION PRESS • NEW YORK

to my husband, Ira —P. L. L.

Library of Congress Cataloging-in-Publication Data

Laskin, Pamela L.
    Wish upon a star : a story for children with a parent who is
mentally ill / by Pamela L. Laskin and Addie Alexander Moskowitz ;
illustrated by Margo Lemieux.
        p.   cm.
    Summary: A little girl tries to adjust to her mother's mental
illness.
    ISBN 0-945354-30-4. — ISBN 0-945354-29-0 (pbk.)
    1. Mentally ill—Juvenile literature.   [1. Mentally ill.]
I. Moskowitz, Addie Alexander.   II. Lemieux, Margo, ill.
III. Title.
RC460.2.L37   1991
155.9'16—dc20   91-211
                                                        CIP
                                                        AC

Distributed in Canada by Book Center, 1140 Beaulac St., Montreal, Quebec H4R 1R8, Canada

Manufactured in the United States of America

10 9 8 7 6 5 4 3 2 1

Introduction for Parents

Mental illness is an isolating experience for families. Frequently, family members feel shame, fear, and resentment of the disturbed spouse, child, parent, or sibling. However, for adults, support can eventually be found in the process of seeking out treatment and services for themselves and their families. Self-help, advocacy, and psychotherapy groups are available and publicly advertised. These can help to ease the isolation and reduce the stigma initially experienced. How comforting it can be to meet another family who has struggled with and perhaps come to terms with a member's mental illness!

For children, however, mental illness in a parent is particularly isolating, confusing, and frightening. In treatment we frequently hear adults share childhood experiences of a parent's psychopathology which was never shared before with anyone. It is all too common to hear how lonely, different, and shamed these children felt.

This book is meant to help young children of a mentally ill parent by providing another child's experience with the same dilemma. It shares the frightening and confusing moments that happen when a child has a parent incapable of parenting. While each child's experience will, of course, be different, all children will find comfort in how this little girl learns to deal with her fears and loneliness aided by other adults in her life.

Parents, relatives, and mental health professionals will find this story to be a wonderful tool to acknowledge and help children cope with the many difficulties in growing up with a mentally ill parent.

My mommy is sick. She's been this way for as long as I remember. She doesn't have a runny nose or a fever, but she doesn't act the way other mommies do.

Mommy can't get my breakfast ready. Daddy makes breakfast. Sometimes he makes my favorite—blueberry pancakes!

Mommy doesn't eat with us. Instead she screams that there's a mess. Sometimes she screams weird things at strangers or at no one at all.

Mommy sits and stares for hours. Sometimes she stays in her pajamas all day long.

Her eyes are beautiful, but she doesn't even look at me. Sometimes I feel invisible since Mommy doesn't look at me. She doesn't touch me, either. I wonder what I did that she won't touch me.

My Daddy says I'm very huggable. We cuddle
all the time. He tells me Mommy would love to
hug me, too, but she can't help herself.

Daddy tells me that Mommy's head is like a car without brakes. She has fast thoughts, but no brakes to stop them.

I giggle thinking that Mommy's head is like a car. But I'm angry, too.

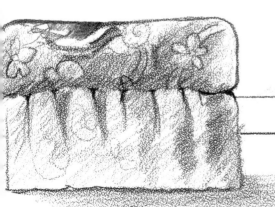

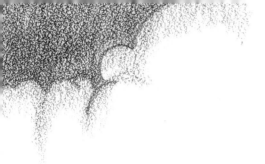

I'm angry Mommy can't pick me up after school,
the way other mommies do.

I'm angry she didn't come to see my dance recital.
Daddy was worried that she'd start to scream.

One time it was my four-year-old birthday. I wore my special party dress. Mommy just walked right past me.

When Mommy takes her medicine, it's like the
brakes Daddy talks about. She seems better for
a while.

But when Mommy doesn't take her medicine, she doesn't notice me at all. I feel like it's my fault. This makes me sad.

I'm even sadder when Mommy has to go to the
hospital. Daddy takes her when she screams too
much. But sometimes I'm so mad at Mommy for
not taking her medicine that I'm glad she's gone.

Then Grandma comes to stay with us. Grandma has the same green eyes as Mommy.

Grandma sings all day long. She smells like the grass and trees. That's because she likes the outdoors so much.

We do fun things together. Grandma is teaching me to crochet. I'll be the only kid in the neighbor-hood who can crochet.

Grandma is the world's greatest cook. We make
oatmeal cookies. Grandma tells me that when
Mommy was little they made oatmeal cookies
together, too.

Grandma makes me laugh. I wish Mommy could
laugh with Grandma and me and Daddy.

I wish Mommy could read me a good-night story.

When Grandma kisses me good-night, we blow kisses out to the stars. Daddy always gives me a gigantic kiss. He says that I can make wishes on a star.

3

I wish that when Mommy comes out of the hospital, she'll be better for always. Daddy says that's a wonderful wish.

Good-night, stars. Good-night Grandma and
Daddy. Good-night, Mommy. Feel better.